HAND–TO–HAND FIGHTING

HAND-TO-HAND FIGHTING

A SYSTEM OF PERSONAL DEFENSE
FOR THE SOLDIER

BY

A. E. MARRIOTT

CAMP PHYSICAL DIRECTOR
ARMY Y. M. C. A., CAMP SEVIER

FOREWORD BY

BENJAMIN S. GROSS
WELFARE DEPARTMENT
CAMP SEVIER, S. C.

PHOTOS POSED BY

C. W. KNEBEL
A. E. MARRIOTT

The Naval & Military Press Ltd

Published by

The Naval & Military Press Ltd

Unit 5 Riverside, Brambleside
Bellbrook Industrial Estate
Uckfield, East Sussex
TN22 1QQ England

Tel: +44 (0)1825 749494

www.naval-military-press.com
www.nmarchive.com

FOREWORD

In an article, "Bayonet Fighting and Physical Training," in the August, 1917, number of the *Infantry Journal*, Major Percy Hobbs of the Canadian Forces writes that "after a bayonet attack, in nine cases out of ten (trench or open), the men grapple. . . . The man who has never been there before, so to speak, doesn't know what to do. He has been shown and practiced in shortening arms and jabbing and dropping his weapon and disarming the other fellow, and a lot of counters and trips and tricks. Well, your average trained men tie themselves up in a knot and roll about on grass and forget everything."

Major Hobbs is but one of the many military writers who have emphasized the vital necessity of every Infantry man knowing what to do when he meets the enemy in a hand-to-hand encounter. Not since the Middle Ages has a knowledge of this method of fighting been so essential as it is to-day. As the great war progresses it is becoming more and more apparent that the expertness and skill of the individual are playing an increasingly large part in the determination of the final outcome.

That events have taken this turn, is perhaps the fortunate thing from the viewpoint of the American soldier. Of all the peoples of the earth the average American is undoubtedly the most experienced and the most apt in hand-to-hand fighting. This is partly the result of his activity in certain sports. Boxing, though frowned upon professionally in the majority of our communities, is after all distinctly an American sport. It is but the natural expression of the native American's instinct of fighting with his fists.

This form of combat has given the inhabitants of the United States a marked advantage in the quick and expert use of the hands. Baseball, the most national of our games, has been especially instrumental in training the American eye and producing suppleness of body. Football has ingrained into our youth a certain gameness and a stick-to-itiveness and has cultivated grit. All are qualities essential to hand-to-hand encounter.

During the third year of the war, when hand-to-hand combats became the rule rather than

the exception, English officers stated that the
enemy was at a distinct disadvantage in such a
fight. As he has seldom been a patron of the
manly sports, the average German in a combat
is clumsy in the use of his hands. Not being
accustomed to baseball, or other games of like
nature, he finds it hard to stand up against a
mass flying in his direction. As a result, almost
every time an Englishman hurled his helmet at
him, the enemy was so upset that before he could
regain his equilibrium he was pierced with the
bayonet. On other occasions, reports have come
from English officers that their men had found
the application of a few jiu-jitsu tricks in grap-
pling to be of great service in vanquishing of
their opponents.

Utilizing the facts embodied in these reports
as a suggestion, this volume presents a series of
positions and holds for the use of the soldier
engaged in hand-to-hand encounter. The object
of this method is two-fold : to disable or destroy
the opponent ; and to defend oneself.

Many of the holds and attacks of the system
are familiar to the followers of the Græco-Roman,
catch-as-catch-can and jiu-jitsu wrestling. These
have been combined and adapted to the need in

hand. In applying them, however, one must not confuse them with like holds in wrestling. The soldier must remember that the latter is a sport whose climax is the placing of a wrestler's shoulders to the mat, while the subject matter of this volume constitutes a deadly system whose climax is nothing less than the destruction or crippling of the opponent. It should be further emphasized that many of the acts barred in clean wrestling are essential parts of the system, and indeed are the most effective means of doing away with an opponent. For instance, the gouging out of a man's eyes or kicking him in the groin would be unheard of in the wrestling game. In this system these are the acts toward which all other things lead. They form the apex, and result, if properly applied, in the destruction of the enemy. To this end every hold and combination of holds has as its object the bringing of the opponent into such a position as to enable the aggressor to attack the eyes or the groin. So painful and so wracking to the nervous system are injuries at these points that the enemy becomes helpless for a sufficient period of time to enable the attacker to destroy him or force his surrender.

This system of destruction and self-defense is so fraught with dire consequence to the enemy that in a man-to-man encounter, where it is the life of one man against the life of the other, the soldier having mastery of it is bound to have an overwhelming advantage. This must be the case especially against an enemy notoriously ineffective in hand-to-hand fighting. The drilling in the various holds and attacks described and illustrated in this manual, therefore, will result not only in development of the soldier's physical attributes and his natural powers of destruction, but will also instill in him a greater confidence and self-reliance in bayonet attack and close-up encounter.

The practicability of this system has already been proven by its adoption by a number of Companies of the 30th Army Division at Camp Sevier, South Carolina. It has developed latent possibilities in the soldiers, and has won the praise of all the officers who have had occasion to observe its effects on the men and to test its efficiency on the drill ground.

In this connection the author of this volume expresses his appreciation to Col. T. K. McCully, 118th Inf., Major G. H. Mahon, 118th Inf., Capt.

W. D. Workman, Co. A, 118th Inf., Capt. Murrah, 12th Co. 55th Depot Brigade, and Capt. F. Hinton, 11th Co. 55th Depot Brigade, as well as other officers, for their helpful suggestions and invaluable assistance in testing the efficacy of this system.

BENJAMIN S. GROSS,
Welfare Department,
Camp Sevier, S. C.

HAND-TO-HAND FIGHTING

PERSONAL DEFENSE

Object:

To use to the fullest extent the physical attributes of every soldier.

To demonstrate to the soldier his powers of defense and destruction.

To instill confidence and self-reliance in attacking the enemy in bayonet and hand-to-hand encounter.

To destroy or disable an opponent. To defend oneself in hand-to-hand encounter with the enemy.

DEFINITIONS

Attention: The position the unarmed soldier assumes upon the command of attention given by the officer.

11

Attack: The command of execution.

Distance: The distance between the front and rear rank, from the back of the men in the front rank to the chest of the men in the rear rank.

Defense: The rank or individual on whom the holds are being applied.

Fistic Attack: The section in which the fists are used similar to boxing; the attack being made from the front.

Foot Work: The use of the foot upon the fallen enemy.

Frontal Attack: The section in which all holds are applied with the individuals or ranks facing each other.

Interval: The distance between men measured from elbow to elbow in rank.

Offense: The rank or individual executing the hold.

On Guard: The command to bring the Company to the starting position in fistic attack.

Rear Attack: The section in which all holds are applied from the rear.

Reverse: Reverse the rank of attack to the rank of defense.

Recover: Return to starting position.

CHIEF POINTS OF ATTACK

1. Eyes   3. Neck
2. Groin   4. 9th Rib

1. **Eyes:** Never miss an opportunity to destroy the eyes of the enemy. **In all head holds use the fingers on the eyes**. They are the most delicate points in the body and easy to reach. The eye can easily be removed with the finger. See Illustrations Nos. 6, 9, 19.

2. **Groin:** The enemy can easily be disabled by a well-directed kick in the groin. Never miss an opportunity to use the knee or the foot. Train yourself to look for an opportunity; as a rule you will always find a chance in bayonet attack or hand-to-hand encounter. See Illustrations Nos. 16, 19, 24, 30, 40, 41.

3. **Neck:** It is easy to strangle a man with any of the neck holds, but the chief weapon of attack for the neck is the foot. Aim to throw your man off his feet and stay on yours. Never give the enemy a chance to recover after he is thrown, but stamp upon the neck with the foot. (See Illustration No. 36.) Don't kick, but jump on it with the full weight of the body.

4. **9th Rib:** The 9th rib as a point of attack is easy to reach when the enemy is thrown upon his back. (See Illustration No. 38.) Stamp upon the ribs about 4 to 6 inches below the nipple. Keep the knee stiff, using the weight of the body. The ribs will crumple under the weight.

Note. — The natural tendency is to kick the fallen enemy. This is not quite as effective as the stamp using the body weight.

TECHNIQUE OF COMPANY INSTRUCTION — PRELIMINARY

The instructor should have four assistants in the preliminary instruction.

The Company forms two squares, one inside the other. The inside square will be termed the Front Rank; the outside square the Rear Rank. The distance between the inside square (Front Rank) and the outside square (Rear Rank) is 24 inches.

The instructor will take his position in the center of the inside square. The assistants will take a position outside the square, one on each side.

The instructor should see that the Rank of Defense does not offer resistance. Preliminary instruction is given to enable large numbers of men to learn the holds of the system and not for combat. The work should be strictly formal.

Individual and Company combative work should be indulged in only when the men are properly equipped.

1. There are two kinds of commands: 1, the preparatory command, which indicates the hold to be executed.   2. The command of execution.

2. The preparatory command will be the name of the hold.   The command of execution will be *attack*.

3. The rank or individual that applies the hold will be termed the *offense*.   The rank upon which the hold is being applied will be termed the *defense*.

4. Upon the command of *recover* the Company will return to the starting position of the hold which is being applied.

5. Upon the command of *reverse* the Company will change the rank of attack to rank of defense.

Rear Attack No. 1 : The Company will assume the position of attention.   Upon the command of execution the rank of attack will step forward upon the left foot, keeping the right foot in place when not used in the holds. Execute the hold and return to starting position upon the command of *Recover*.

Frontal Attack No. 2: The front rank facing the rear rank 24 inches apart, the soldier at position of attention. Upon the command of execution, the rank of attack will step forward upon the left foot, keeping the right in place when not used in executing the hold, returning to starting position upon command of *Recover*.

Fistic Attack No. 3: Front rank facing the rear rank 24 inches apart. Upon command of *On Guard* front rank and rear rank take one step forward (about 12 inches) with the left foot, assuming the boxer's position. Left arm forward; right arm across front chest. Upon command of execution Company will attack. Return to starting position (boxer's position) after attack without command.

Note. — The left foot must be in place at all times in the Company instruction. The instructor will find difficulty in this section unless this point is rigidly enforced. After the men are well schooled the knee groin kick, etc., with the left leg can be used.

Ground Work No. 4 : Company will assume position of attention. Upon command of *Ground Position* the front rank will drop to the hands and knees ; the rear rank will step forward, place the right foot between the legs of the opponent, drop to the left knee (knee slightly to the left of the opponent's left knee) keeping the trunk erect. The Company will execute the hold and return to this position upon command of *Recover*.

Foot Work No. 5 : This attack cannot be given in Company formation. The instruction should be informal ; demonstrated and practiced upon a dummy.

Neck Attack No. 6 : Stamp upon the neck with the foot ; keep the leg straight, throwing the whole weight of the body into the attack. See Illustration No. 36 and 37.

Note. — Don't bend the knee or kick at the enemy in the attack.

9th Rib Attack : Stamp upon the ribs 4 to 6 inches below the nipple, using the stiff

knee and weight of the body as in neck attack.   See Illustration No. 38.

Note. — The groin and solar plexus can be at-
tacked in the same manner, but the neck and 9th
rib are the chief points of attack and more effective.

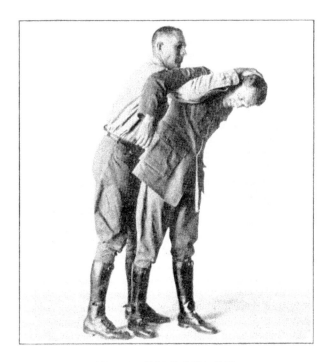

NO. 1. HALF NELSON

Place the upper arm in the arm-pit of the enemy; bend the forearm, placing the hand on the back of the head, lifting under the arm with downward pressure on the head.

Note. The hand should be placed high on the head and not on the back of the neck.

NO. 2. FULL NELSON

This hold is the double of No. 1 (HALF NELSON). Place
both arms in the arm-pits of the enemy with the hands on
the back of the head; fingers slightly interlocked. Downward pressure on the head, slight upward lift under the arms.

NO. 3. REAR STRANGLE HOLD

Throw the right arm around the opponent's neck, the forearm close up against the throat; place the other arm over the shoulder; grab the left arm firmly just above the elbow; place the left hand upon the back of the head, pulling backward upon the right arm, forcing the forearm against the neck. Apply pressure upon the head with the left hand, downward and forward.

NO. 1. BAR LOCK

Throw the right arm around the neck, the forearm against the throat, and the left upper-arm over the left shoulder. Grasp the left upper-arm with the right hand, just above the elbow. Place the left forearm in back of neck, grasping the upper right arm with the left hand about at the biceps. Apply pressure backward with the right and push forward with the left arm.

NO. 5. HAMMER LOCK

Grab the wrist of the opponent and with a quick backward pull force the forearm up the back toward the head. Continue until dislocated.

Note. In photo forward trip is also shown.

NO. 6. HIP BREAK

Catch the opponent by the head USING THE FINGERS TO GOUGE THE EYES. Pull the head backward with a snap. Thrust the foot forward, toe turned out, striking the hock of the knee and forcing the knee to the ground. As the knee strikes the ground, throw all of your weight on the head and shoulders of the enemy, pushing forward and downward.

NO. 7. KIDNEY KICK

Catch hold of the opponent's head (USING THE FINGERS ON THE EYES), pull the head backward with a snap, at the same time striking the enemy sharply in the back with the knee. FINISH up with the HIP BREAK, bring the foot downward and forward, striking the hock of the knee, forcing the knee to the ground. When the knee strikes the ground, throw all of your weight on the head and shoulders, pushing forward and downward until the opponent is disabled.

NO. 8. BODY THROW

Place both arms around the enemy just above the hips.
Lift him off his feet with a sharp, quick jerk, swinging the
head toward the ground and the feet sideward and upward.
Throw the enemy violently to the ground, following up with
the foot work before he has time to recover.

NO. 9. HEAD TWIST

Strike the opponent under the chin with the heel of the right hand, and continue the thrust, twisting the head to the right, sideward and upward. Place the palm of the left hand upon the top of the head with the fingers just above the ear. Pull the top of the head to the left and push the chin to the right.

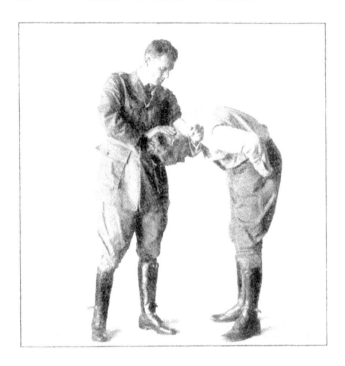

NO. 10. FRONT STRANGLE

With the left forearm against the neck of the opponent,
the right hand back of the head, push downward with the
right and lift upward against the neck with the left forearm.

NO. 11. CHANCERY HOLD

Catch the opponent's head between the upper right arm and the trunk (body), bringing the forearm across the front of the face. To add to the pressure, use the forearm as a lever, pulling it against the face by grasping the right hand or wrist with the left and pulling it upward.

NO. 12. UNDER ARM BREAK

Easily secured when the enemy reaches for a gun or knife;
grasp the wrist of the opponent; push the upper arm to a
level with the shoulder, the forearm at right angles. With
the free hand grasp the elbow, pulling it forward sharply,
at the same time force the wrist backward.

NO. 13. OVER ARM BREAK

This hold is used in warding off overhand knife attack.
Side step slightly, grasp the wrist and elbow of the opponent,
push the wrist back, and at the same time pull the elbow
forward sharply. If possible force the enemy backward
to the ground and use the foot work.

NO. 14. WRIST BREAK

Grasp the right elbow of the opponent with the left hand and his left hand with your right, with his arm in a flexed position, force the elbow upward and press down on the back of the hand.

Note. Opening for this break in overhead knife attack and boxer's offensive position, etc.

NO. 15. ELBOW BREAK

Grasp the wrist, turning the palm of the hand upward, and strike a sharp blow under the elbow; at the same time pull down violently upon the wrist.

D

NO. 16. KNEE GROIN KICK

Raise the knee, strike violently in the groin. An excellent means of disabling the opponent.

NO. 17. FOREARM AND CROTCH HOLD

Strike the opponent violently under the chin with the left forearm, forcing the head backward toward the ground. With the right in the crotch, give a forward upward lift and throw the enemy backward.

NO. 18.   ARM THRUST AND BELT HOLD

Catch hold of the belt or clothing at the waist line with the right hand, striking the opponent under the chin with the heel of the left hand, and continue the thrust, forcing the head backward.   Pull the opponent forward at the waist, arching the back, force him backward to the ground.

NO. 19. ARM THRUST AND BACK HOLD

Strike the opponent violently under the chin with the heel of the hand and continue the thrust backward, at the same time place the other hand behind the back and pull him toward you, arching the back. Throw backward to the ground; while the enemy is falling, use the knee groin kick.

NO. 20. FLYING BUTTOCK

Place the right arm around the neck of the opponent. Turn the back, bend forward, extending the hip to the right, pull down upon the head, at the same time give a quick upward hitch, throwing the enemy over the hip.

NO. 21. FLYING MARE

Grasp the arm of the opponent, turn the palm of the hand up, keeping the arm straight. Turn your back upon the enemy, placing his arm over your right shoulder. Place your shoulder in the arm-pit; lift upward, at the same time bending forward with a quick jerky motion, throwing the opponent over head.

NO. 22. HIGH RIGHT SWING AND LEAD FOR
THE JAW

As the opponent swings with his right, block with the left
forearm and lead for the jaw with your right. Follow in
with the knee groin kick if possible.

Note. In the entire boxing series, the chief point of
attack is the groin.

NO. 23. STRAIGHT LEFT, RIGHT LEAD FOR THE BODY

As the opponent leads a straight left for the head, slip the head to the right, lead to the body with your left. Follow with the groin kick if opening.

NO. 24. STRAIGHT LEFT LEAD AND GROIN
KICK

Lead for the face with a straight left. As the opponent
covers or ducks, raise the left knee to the groin.

NO. 25. DUCK UNDER, LEFT LEAD FOR BODY

As the opponent leads with a right swing, duck under it and lead for the body with your left. As you recover, use the toe groin kick if possible.

NO. 26—DUCK UNDER, GROIN LEAD

When the opponent leads a straight right for the head, duck under it and attack the groin with your right. In recovering, an opportunity for the knee or toe groin kick may present itself.

NO. 27. INSTEP AND HEART LEAD

Stamp on the instep of the opponent with your left foot, leading for the heart with your right.

Note. Care should be taken in this attack, as a slight blow from the enemy's right may floor you.

NO. 28. RIGHT PIN AND LEAD FOR BODY

Pin down the left arm of your opponent between your upper arm and body. Lead for the body with your right. Follow up with the knee groin kick.

NO. 29. ARM PIN AND KNEE GROIN KICK

Shows the arm pin of No. 28 with the knee groin kick.

NO. 30. TOE GROIN KICK

Knock down the guard of the opponent with your left arm and follow up with the left toe to the groin.

NO. 31. HALF NELSON AND LEG PIN

For a description of Half Nelson see Illustration No. 1. LEG PIN: Kneeling on the left knee, place the right foot in between the legs of the opponent, keeping the heel close to the near knee of the opponent, or the right foot can be placed upon leg of the opponent just above the calf.

E

NO. 32. HALF NELSON HAMMER LOCK AND
LEG PIN

For description, see Half Nelson, No. 1, Hammer Lock,
No. 5, and Leg Pin, No. 31.

NO. 33. TOE HOLD

Place the left knee half way between the hip and the knee of the opponent, grasp the toe with the right hand, twisting it inward as you push the leg upward toward the back.

Note. This hold can also be applied in the standing position by placing the foot upon the thigh of opponent in place of the knee.

NO. 34.   HEAD SCISSORS AND HAMMER LOCK

Catch the head of your opponent between your legs about half way between the knees and the crotch.   Cross the legs, locking them at the ankles.   Apply pressure by trying to touch the knees together and straightening out the legs with the ankles locked. Grasp the wrist of the enemy with your free hand, apply the hammer lock.

NO. 35. RUNNING TRIP

This hold will throw the opponent when he is running, or it can be used at any time that the foot is off the ground and can be readily grasped. Catch hold of the foot at the instep or ankle and pull the leg sideward and upward with a snap, throwing the enemy to the ground. Follow up with foot work

NO. 36. NECK STAMP FRONT

Jump quickly to the near side of the fallen opponent, shift the body weight momentarily to the leg farthest from his head, spring forward, landing on the neck under the chin with the other foot, keeping the leg stiff and throwing all of the weight onto the stamping foot.

NO. 37. NECK STAMP REAR

Attack same as No. 36 on the back of the neck, used when the enemy is thrown face down.

NO. 38.   RIB ATTACK

Stamp upon the ribs about 4 to 6 inches below the nipple.
Attack same as No. 36 (Neck Stamp).

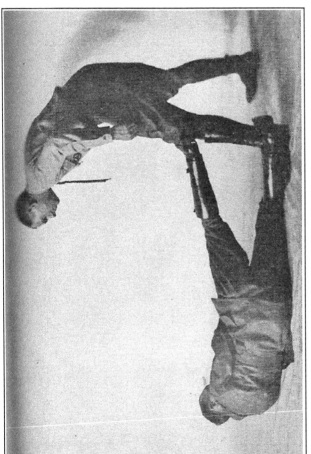

NO. 39. LEG THROW

When thrown to the ground near the opponent, turn onto the side, raise up on the elbow, hook the toe of the under foot in back of the heel or ankle of the enemy, draw up the top leg and kick the enemy violently upon the knee with the heel or instep of the foot.

NO. 30.   LAYING GROIN KICK

If the enemy is over you astride, draw up the knee, drive the heel or instep to the groin.

NO. 11. ON SIDE, TOE GROIN KICK

If thrown to the ground, roll onto the side, raise up on the elbow, and kick the enemy in

NO. 42. SITTING KNEE BREAK

Grasp the ankle or heel of the opponent with one hand and the toe with the other; place the heel or instep of the foot on the outside of the knee; force the knee inward with the foot and pull outward on the ankle and the toe with the hands.

NO. 43. BACKWARD TRIP

Place your foot in back of the enemy (firmly on the ground), push the opponent violently backward.

Note. The foot can be placed outside or inside the leg of the opponent.

NO. 44. FRONT TRIP

Same as the backward trip (see Backward Trip, No. 43) with the foot placed in front of the enemy and the push from the back.

COMBINATIONS

Some of the holds applied independently are not very effective. It is therefore necessary to use them in combination to secure the best results. The instructor should see that the soldier is well schooled in this work.

Arm Thrust and Belt Hold	Knee Groin Kick. Backward Trip.
Arm Thrust and Back Hold	Knee Groin Kick. Backward Trip.
Bar Lock	No Combinations.
Body Throw	No Combinations.
Chancery Hold	No Combinations.
Elbow Break	Groin Kick — Toe. Groin Kick — Knee. Backward Trip.
Flying Buttock	No Combinations.
Flying Mare	No Combinations.
Forearm and Crotch	Backward Trip.
Front Strangle	Groin Kick — Toe.
Full Nelson	No Combinations.
Hammer Lock	Half Nelson. Forward Trip. Head Scissors.

Half Nelson	Forward Trip. Hammer Lock. Leg Pin.
Head Twist	Backward Trip. Groin Kick — Knee.
Kidney Kick	No Combinations.
Knee Groin Kick	Use whenever in close enough with any hold.
Over Arm Break	Knee Groin Kick. Backward Trip.
Running Trip	No Combinations.
Scissors	Hammer Lock.
Strangle from the Rear	No Combinations.
Under Arm Break	Knee Groin Kick. Toe Groin Kick.
Wrist Break	Front Trip. Rear Trip. Groin Kick — Knee.

Note. The Combinations above are advised. Other Combinations can be used, but in doing so the soldier gives his opponent an advantage.

In the entire Boxing Series the Groin Kicks and Backward Trip are the only Combinations advised.

POSITIONS

Starting position in the **Rear Attack**.
Illustration No. 45.

Starting position in **Frontal Attack**.
Illustration No. 46.

Starting position in the **Fistic Attack**.
Illustration No. 47.

Starting position in the **Ground Work**.
Illustration No. 48.

NO. 45.

NO. 46.

NO. 48.

PERSONAL DEFENSE INSTRUCTION AT CAMP SEVIER

Illustrations Nos. 49-50-51-52-53-54. Officers of the 118th Infantry receiving instruction in Personal Defense — A. E. Marriott, Instructor.

Illustrations Nos. 55-56-57-58: Company Instruction, 11th and 12th Companies, 3d Training Battalion, 55th Depot Brigade, Capts. Hinton and Murrah commanding — C. W. Knebel, Instructor.

NO. 49.

NO. 50

No. 52.

NO. 53.

No. 54.

NO. 55.

NO. 57.

CPSIA information can be obtained
at www.ICGtesting.com
Printed in the USA
LVHW010920300623
751245LV00001B/1

9 781474 537728